Pre-K **3**

Family

Contents

 Look and put the sticker.

grandpa

mom

puppy

sister

Put sticker on the word.

Hi, Mom .

Hi.

Say.

✏️ **Color and say.**

 grandpa

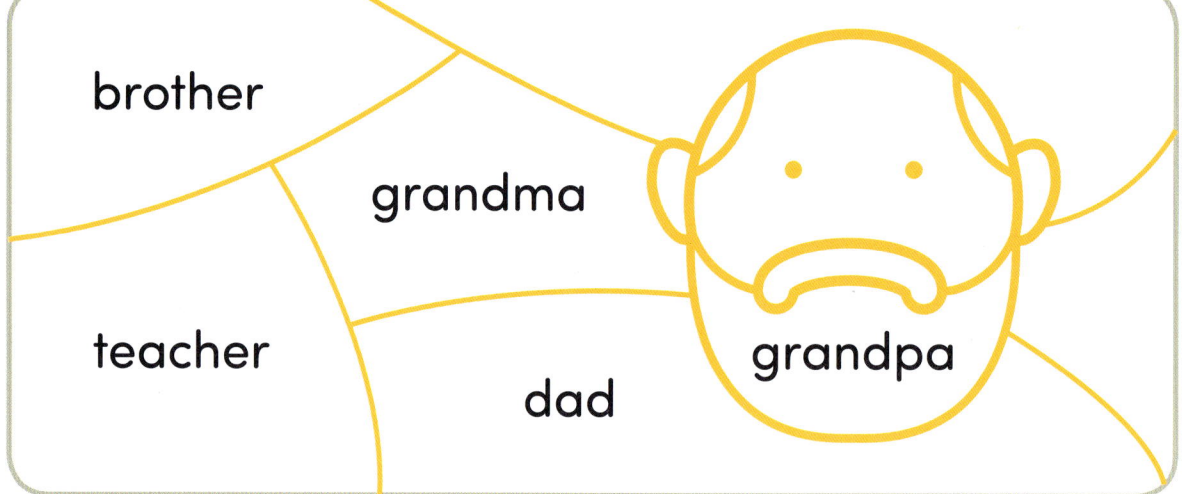

brother

grandma

teacher

dad

grandpa

 sister

grandpa

sister

mom

dad

puppy

 Look and put the sticker.

brother

teacher

grandma

dad

 **Put sticker on the word.**

Hi, Dad .

Hi.

 **Say.**

p. 2

 p. 3

Mom

 p. 5

 p. 6

Dad

Sticker

 Good work!
 Wonderful work!
 Great effort!
 For working hard!

 Good work!
Excellent!
Well done!
Well done!
Special award!

Find and circle.

mom

grandpa

 Put the people in the house.

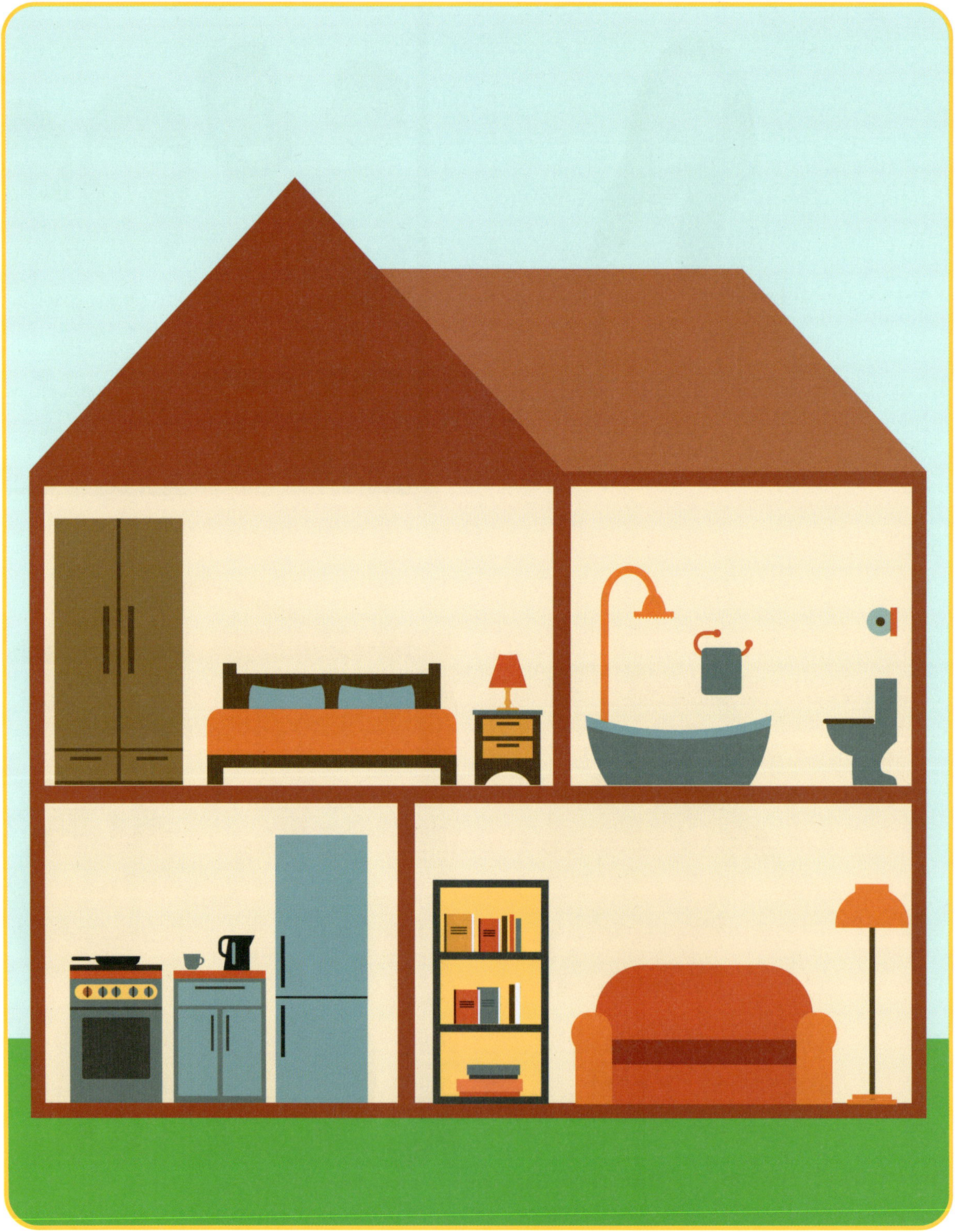

dad	mom
grandpa	grandma

brother	sister
puppy	teacher